# CANCER DIAGNOSIS

## 30 Tips to Help You Land on Your Feet

# CANCER DIAGNOSIS

## 30 Tips to Help You Land on Your Feet

Rick Bergh, M.Div., CT

Author of *Taking Notice* and *Looking Ahead*

Cancer Diagnosis: 30 Tips to Help You Land on Your Feet

Copyright © 2015 by Rick Bergh

Published by
Beacon Mount Publishing
18 West Chapman Place
Cochrane, Alberta, T4C 1J9, Canada
www.rickbergh.com   www.beaconmountpublishing.com

ISBN 978-1-988082-25-7 (paperback)

This publication is not intended as a substitute for the advice of health care professionals.

Printed and bound in the United States of America.

# Dedication

This book is dedicated to my mom. When my dad was diagnosed with cancer, Mom stood by him, even when it wasn't easy. The two of them engaged life fully – together. They did it with joy, hope and love and taught me the importance of commitment even in the tough times. Thanks, Mom, for being such an inspiration.

# Acknowledgements

This book was written as a supplement to *Finding Anchors: How to Bring Stability to Your Life Following a Cancer Diagnosis.*

Not everyone enjoys reading large amounts of printed material. Often a small portion of information is all we need to help us get our footing. This book is intended to give a brief overview of things to consider following a cancer diagnosis.

I want to thank my wife, Erica, for being the frontrunner on this project. She was my primary editor and provided amazing feedback for this work.

Of course, I always acknowledge my "teachers" – those individuals and clients with whom I've worked over the past 30 years. They are the inspiration behind many of these tips.

This book came about as a result of reading *Proverbs* in the Bible. It amazed me how short statements could encourage, challenge and edify. It made me realize how much I needed the insight from these words to start each day.

# Preface

You are reading this book because you are being intentional in your journey. This may be the hardest transition in your life to date, but you are willing to wrestle with it and land on your feet.

I once found myself at the edge of a cliff. There was water below. The precipice was high and I was supposed to jump. No one was waiting below. Just water – and I wondered if there was something below the surface. To jump into thin air, where I'd be out of control, seemed frightening to me. I did it, but I must admit that it felt good to step onto the shore and put my feet on solid ground once again.

A cancer diagnosis might feel like you're free falling, wondering where you will land. Here are some tips for you to consider "in the jump". There are 30 of them – one for each day of the month.

You will land on your feet!

# Contents

# Telling Others

> *Live your life from your heart. Share from your heart.*
> *And your story will touch and heal people's souls.*
> —MELODY BEATTIE

Every time you tell your story you become stronger. It's exhausting at the outset, but telling others reminds them (and you) of your resolve to live. It says, "I have an obstacle in my life but I'm moving forward." It says, "I have cancer but I expect it to be a temporary bump in the road."

No one believes that they will ever be diagnosed with cancer, but when it happens, it feels surreal and isolates you. You feel alienated, wondering how much you should share with others or even if you should mention it at all. In my experience, it is better to tell people about your diagnosis than to keep silent and suffer alone.

What's the best way to do that? I always recommend that people write out a script of how they will tell their story to others. It may not sound very personal or spontaneous, but if you know what you are going to say ahead of time, it helps to reduce the emotional load and diminishes your sense of vulnerability.

People are naturally curious and want details — most people are natural busy bodies. Decide what details you want to share and don't waiver. You don't have to respond to every question they might have. Just tell them what you would like to share and leave it at that.

Whether in person, on the phone or in a text, write down what you plan to say and stick to it. Less is more.

It really helps!

# Naming the
# Emotion

**30**

*Your intellect may be confused, but your
emotions will never lie to you.*

—ROGER EBERT

A re your emotions running wild? It's okay—you're normal. Don't pretend to be super human. You've just received some very difficult news and you are trying to sort through what's happening. You are pre-occupied with significant concerns, wondering how your present situation will affect your future.

Does this ring true for you?

As difficult as it may seem, don't allow your emotions to run roughshod over you. If you are someone who tends to process information with your feelings, you may find this challenging. Feelings need to be recognized for their important role in your life—they are telling you something that you need to hear and should be examined in that light.

Every feeling is fair and morally neutral. So it's important to recognize an emotion, name it and understand what it's telling you about what steps you need to take. Don't be embarrassed by or ashamed of it. You may be surprised where it will lead you. An emotion can simmer for a while in order to process it, but don't sit in it for too long without sharing it with another person. Letting someone else know what you are experiencing is the best way to diffuse anxiety.

# DAY 3:
## Dealing with Disbelief

*What do you know? Haven't you heard
of suspension of disbelief?*

— ED WOOD

"This can't be happening to me!" You have likely either spoken this phrase or at least thought it.

Not only have you probably said this, but those closest to you are saying it as well. Maybe not out loud, but they are thinking it, for sure. It's only normal.

Shock and disbelief are a normal response in this transition. Some days, you will accept your reality and work with it; other days, it will feel like a bad dream. Emotional whiplash is normal initially.

This is not an end. It is a beginning. You will settle into the reality that you have cancer and so will your family and friends. Then you will be able to make some important decisions to stabilize your life and move forward.

Be patient. Know that for the moment, you have cancer. It is not a final chapter. Live life fully as though you didn't have cancer—don't let it dictate whether you can live in a joy-filled place. It can only steal from you what you allow it to steal.

Someday it will be a story, told in past tense.

# DAY 4:
# Confronting Exhaustion

**30**

*Follow effective action with quiet reflection. From the quiet reflection will come even more effective action.*

—PETER DRUCKER

A re you exhausted both emotionally and physically? You've been telling people about your cancer diagnosis and meeting with doctors. You have so many fears and concerns and are just trying to keep things on an even keel. You just want everything to slow down for a moment.

What do you do with *tired*? How do you live with *exhausting*?

Make a list of everything that is overwhelming you... and then forget about it for a day.

You're exhausted because you're overwhelmed. Put it aside for one day and rest. No phone calls. No visitors. No talking.

Make a to-do list and place it aside for this day. Honestly—everything can wait.

Refresh yourself by doing nothing, thinking nothing, feeling nothing.

Just breathe. Relax. Rest you mind. Be kind to yourself.

# DAY 5:
# Reworking Fear

*The oldest and strongest emotion of mankind
is fear, and the oldest and strongest kind
of fear is fear of the unknown.*

—H.P. LOVECRAFT

I t's not easy to live without fear when you have cancer. You might be worried about the outcome or prognosis. You might be fearful about the future. You may be thinking about your treatments, family members or even your finances.

Today, make a list of all your fears and ask if there is anything you can do about any of them. If you can, take action. If not, then cross them off with a big "X".

Don't let something you can't control take away your joy.

How might you do this?

- Give it to God
- Tell it to leave

- Share it with a friend
- Decide that what you can't control has no value in your thought life

Take some action and confront your fear today. Become fear-less.

DAY 6:

# Checking In

Today, check in with your loved ones who are most worried about you.

Your cancer journey impacts those around you in a significant way. You are not alone in this.

Those closest to you are wondering how you are managing, although they may be afraid to ask you. They may be frightened to say something that they shouldn't, so they make small talk or inject humor into the conversation in an attempt to lighten things up.

Family and friends may not know what to say or do, not having encountered something like this before. So you might need to take some initiative. Here's how to help them:

You need to start the conversation with them. Open up the lines of communication. It's not difficult but it is brave. You can begin with: "I just want to check in with you—are you worried about the future like I am?"

That's an honest and open question that leads to a deeper conversation.

# DAY 7:
## Choosing Gratitude

*Gratitude is the fairest blossom*
*which springs from the soul.*
— HENRY WARD BEECHER

It's not easy to find the good in life when you are weighed down. Cancer can feel like a downward vortex, but gratitude will help you gain perspective and manage your circumstances.

Gratitude? Really? Every opportunity to be grateful will keep you afloat. If you look for the bad, you will find the bad readily enough. If you look for the good – expect a flood of goodness. I'm not saying that cancer is good—it isn't. But there are still things that bring joy into your life if you allow them in:

- Does a grandchild's smile melt your heart?
- Does a family that loves you bring you a sense of belonging?
- Does a beautiful sunrise fill you with overwhelming beauty?

Name all those things that are wonderful in your life, no matter how small – anything that is good and positive. Speak them out loud. Tell someone how blessed you are.

Experience how gratitude empowers you to face your circumstance differently.

# DAY 8:
# Establishing Boundaries

*The art of leadership is saying no, not saying yes. It is very easy to say yes.*
—TONY BLAIR

Practice saying *no* today. Perhaps you already have good boundaries—they are essential when you are going through something this significant—but if you aren't good at saying *no*, then you need to practice.

It is your responsibility to set boundaries and decide whom you want to interact with during your cancer journey. It is also your job to clearly tell people what you need (and what you don't need) in the days that follow your cancer diagnosis. It may seem backwards to tell people what you need, but really most people don't know what you need so you'll want to let them know. You may think it's obvious, but people aren't mind readers and need to be told graciously.

You may be surprised by who shows up to help you when the chips are down. Conversely, you may be amazed by who doesn't step up to the plate.

Choose a friend whom you want to be part of your cancer journey and ask them if they would be willing to commit to this role.

If there are some people who have a tendency to interfere or bull-doze and you don't want them around, find an advocate who will act as a buffer. It's not always easy to tell people that you don't want their help, but right now this is what you need to do. You can appreciate them — from a distance! It's your journey and yours to captain.

# DAY 9:
# Revisiting Work

*The relationships we have with people are extremely important to success on and off the job.*
—ZIG ZIGLAR

Have you been thinking about work lately? If you enjoy your job, you are probably wondering about its place in your life right now. Have you communicated with your co-workers or at least to your colleagues who are closest to you? Maybe you're afraid to – you don't want them to label you or worse, replace you.

If you have not spoken to your boss or the human resource department yet, then you need to do so. Ask your boss for the opportunity to speak with those who are closest to you at work. They are probably concerned for you. They are an important part of your life as you have likely spent close to 40 hours a week with them.

By talking to your boss about your requirements (taking time off work for treatments, for example), you are sharing with them this significant shift in your life and you are letting them know how they might be part of your ongoing journey. Those at your workplace are wondering how best to support you. Conversations with your colleagues and your boss are important to have sooner rather than later.

# Implementing Exercise

*Take care of your body. It's the only
place you have to live in.*
—ANONYMOUS

Your body is so complex and although it is struggling with an unwanted intruder, your body is still working to heal itself. Exercise is important – very important in fact.

There are numerous benefits to exercise. Even if you have to take into account your limitations right now, there are still things that you can do that are beneficial.

Exercise helps you…

- think more clearly
- feel and express emotions more clearly
- build up your confidence
- engage in community and interact with others
- become physically stronger in order to fight the disease

Do some form of exercise every day and if you are having a hard time disciplining yourself, invite a friend along to motivate you.

You will notice the difference. Guaranteed.

# DAY 11:
# Finding Your Voice

*The only thing a cat worries about is what's happening right now. As we tell the kittens, you can only wash one paw at a time.*

—LLOYD ALEXANDER

It's tiring to communicate with the many people who are concerned about you. You probably have extended family and friends who don't live nearby and who are waiting to know what's going on with you. It's a legitimate concern for them.

You would like to be able to talk to each of them, but after a while, it gets to be too much.

Today, make a list of all those people with whom you need to communicate. Prioritize your list, beginning with the people you need to speak to personally. Then ask a family member or a friend to communicate with those remaining on your list.

That's smart and saves you a lot of energy.

# DAY 12:
# Using Symbols

*Symbols are the imaginative signposts of life.*
—MARGOT ASQUITH

We love symbols, not in and of themselves but because of the meaning we attach to them. You have important symbols in your home right now whether you realize it or not. They are often placed in a prominent location and remind you of a significant event or person. Perhaps the symbol was a special gift from someone, given to you during an important juncture in your life.

An angel, a cross, a teddy bear, a rock, a piece of jewelry, a special picture or even a piece of furniture—symbols are used to remind us to have hope or to inspire us in some way when life is tough.

Today, you are invited to choose a symbol that will be important to you during your cancer journey. Go buy one or choose something in your home that has significance to you already, or even create something new, if you are so inclined. Talk to your family about the importance of this symbol. It might sit in the middle of the table when you gather together to eat, or be placed in a prominent place in your living room or on the bedside table.

One Holocaust survivor saw a blade of wheat still standing after the field in his concentration camp had been mown — he took refuge in that symbol and kept that blade of wheat, which had given him hope in his dark days in Auschwitz. He survived, just like that wheat. He was still standing after the Holocaust.

Choose the symbol today and begin to attach meaning to it.

## DAY 13:
# Calling a Friend

**30**

*A true friend never gets in your way unless you happen to be going down.*
—ARNOLD H. GLASGOW

F riendship is a very important part of our life - we all need close friends, no matter who we are. There are different kinds of friends.

Many people have numerous acquaintances, those whom they work or socialize with in a community setting. Others have friends they catch up with over coffee once in a while – friends who have been part of their lives in some way in the past because of a common experience. Fewer people seem to have a best friend whom they can count on. This seems especially true for the male population. I say that because I specialize in counseling men and find it to be quite true in most cases.

You only have so much time and emotional energy to invest in relationships. Today, why not invite one friend over and let them know how you are doing and how they can be involved with you during your cancer journey.

Families are key in your life, but sometimes you will need a friend, outside your family, who will listen to you and talk with you. Be mindful that you will need someone who is willing to listen more than talk.

You need someone who is a constant in your life—someone you can count on every week.

Let your family know who this person is and why it is important for you to spend time with them during your cancer journey.

# DAY 14:
# Eating Right

*Once you get into a routine of eating healthy, it hurts twice as much when you fall off the wagon.*
—CARRIE UNDERWOOD

We need to eat and drink — it's a big part of life. One of the dangers of any loss is the possibility of slipping into poor eating habits for convenience's sake. Binge eating and drinking have often been used as a coping mechanism. You don't need to do that and you can put things into place that will help you avoid bad habits.

Today is a new day — get rid of all unhealthy foods in your home that have high sugar and fat content. If it's not available, it will be easier to avoid. I'm not suggesting that you give up life's pleasures, but consider what goes into your mouth and why. Find healthy substitutes. You might consider asking a nutritionist to help you with this.

Experts say that a habit can be changed by continued discipline and good choices made over a period of 3 weeks. Put a chart up on your fridge and invite your family members to be part of this change in your life. Write down every single snack that you enjoy and have family hold you accountable. You will begin to feel better just by creating good eating habits.

What you take into your body makes a difference.

# DAY 15:
# De-Cluttering Your Environment

*The more I examine the issue of clutter, the more effort I put into combating it, because it really does act as a weight.*

—GRETCHEN RUBIN

There are likely some things that have been put on the back burner since your diagnosis: paper work to be sorted, bills to be paid, laundry to be done, a garage to be organized. Living in a cluttered environment can create stress and cause you to feel even more out of control.

You have more than your share of emotional clutter right now. The last few days have been spent sorting out feelings and prioritizing things in your life.

Today, take some time to de-clutter your physical surroundings. You don't have to do it all in one day. Depending upon your energy and time, do just one thing to improve your living environment.

You will be surprised how much better you feel when your surroundings are organized.

# DAY 16:
## Doing What's Important to You

*A morning coffee is my favorite way of starting the day, settling the nerves so that they don't later fray.*
— MARCIA CARRINGTON

There is great value in routine. When life seems unstable and new information is coming at you like shrapnel, maintaining familiar patterns in your daily life is important.

If you normally go out with a friend for coffee every Saturday morning, continue to go.

If you are in an art club and it's important to you, don't give it up.

If reading the morning newspaper is part of your routine, keep reading.

If going to a faith community has been a weekly habit, keep attending.

If Friday is pizza and movie night with your family, stick with it.

Things that are familiar to you give you a sense that, despite constant change, your life is really not out of control. In transition, it's really important to be able to put one foot on solid ground even though the ground under the other foot is shifting.

# Sleeping Patterns

**30**

*It is a common experience that a problem difficult at night is resolved in the morning after the committee of sleep has worked on it.*

—JOHN STEINBECK

When diagnosed with cancer, there are numerous things going on in your head. You are likely worried about the many unknowns that you face up ahead.

In order to process all this new information, both your body and your mind need rest. Lack of sleep can lead to unhealthy side effects like poor judgment, burnout, and depression. You want to eliminate the movement of sadness into depression. It's okay to be sad, but don't let it escalate into something more than it needs to be.

Good sleep is important and necessary for healing and for overcoming both physical and mental stress. It aids in emotional management. When you have a good sleep, you wake up less anxious and are able to start the day with energy that is necessary to face the day.

Here are some things to monitor if you want to rest your whole being, body, soul and mind. These are things that will affect your sleep patterns just before you go to bed:

- the last thing you watch on TV or the internet
- the last thing you read
- the last beverage you drink
- the last conversation you have
- the last music you listen to
- the "need" to go on social media
- the "need" to monitor your incoming phone messages

Two things that I've found particularly helpful in my own life have been:

1   Writing down what I need to do the following day before I fall asleep — it allows me to let go of what's pressing and gives my mind a rest.

2   Saying a prayer and thanking God for all the good things in my life.

You may want to explore what works best for you and try different things — but at the very least, don't underestimate the power of routine in your sleep pattern. You will notice the difference.

# Incorporating Rituals

*We don't have too much ritual in our life anymore.
And these life symbols which people rely on to
keep their feeling of well being, that life is not too
bad after all, are required more and more.*

—JOHN HENCH

Rituals help us recognize moments of transition. They bring community together and allow people to mark significant events with each other.

Rituals like birthdays, anniversaries, graduation, marriage, funerals, baptisms and bar mitzvahs are often understood as rites of passage. When you consider each of these events, they are celebrations that have both a beginning and an end.

Rituals in cancer are no different - they help us to recognize that we have made it this far. We will take many new steps in this journey and each step needs to be celebrated.

Whether big or small, with family or a friend—celebration is empowering. These rituals give life. Decide now what you will do when you make it through a tough time. Decide with whom you will celebrate and make it a shared ritual. It could be as simple as:

- I'm going to celebrate with a glass of wine.
- When I finish my last treatment, I'm going to throw a party for my family and friends.
- When I get through this tough week of treatments, I'm going to book into a hotel and enjoy a weekend with my spouse.
- I'm going to celebrate my "all clear" by having a spa day with my best friend.

You decide what's most helpful for you and get your family and friends involved.

## DAY 19:
# Feeling Sadness

*I have learned now that while those who speak about one's miseries usually hurt, those who keep silence hurt more.*

—C. S. LEWIS

I'm not surprised that you experience some days of sadness. The uncertainty both for you and for your family is palpable. It's a lot for you to take in and sadness is a common response.

You need to visit that place once in awhile. Saying "hello" to the feelings of sadness and then "goodbye" to them are important bookends for moving forward. Both of these involve not just words but actions and emotional decisions as well. Hello and goodbye are both important steps in sadness.

You might be tempted to remain upbeat all the time for the sake of your loved ones, but pretending isn't helpful. If you don't admit to the sadness, then you can't say goodbye to it either. You are only human. You have feelings.

Why are you sad? Reflect upon that for a bit and then tell a friend.

You don't need to figure it all out or have another person give you advice as to how to overcome those feelings — they are normal. Say to your friend, "I just need to let someone know that I'm sad today and why."

And then when you are ready, say goodbye to your sadness for the time being and let go of it.

# Using Schedules

*If you don't know where you are going,*
*you might wind up someplace else.*
—YOGI BERRA

Whether or not you are a "scheduling" type or not, it's helpful to plan ahead—what adjustments will you need to make in your life as you move into this cancer journey initially? If you are going through treatments, surgery and recovery, you will have neither the energy nor the time that you once had. You'll need to make some important changes and decisions as you prioritize your time.

Do your best to build flexibility into your plans as there can be unexpected or unpredictable events thrown in as well. A simple calendar can help you to organize your thoughts on paper and give you rest from thinking about what is ahead. I like to differentiate between planning and control. You can't control everything that happens to you, but you can look ahead and predict to the best of your ability what you might need to have in place for your own sanity.

What could be included in your calendar?
- Medical appointments
- Recovery days
- Quiet times
- Family times
- Connecting with friends
- Activities that are life giving
- Time with your spouse or partner
- Exercise — mild to moderate

You may not follow your schedule to the letter, but it will give you a sense of knowing where you are headed by having some components in place.

**DAY 21:**

# Starting Fresh

*People may hear your words, but they feel your attitude.*

—JOHN C. MAXWELL

The first few times that you meet people following a cancer diagnosis are not easy. They don't know what to say to you, and you are not certain how to respond to them. It's easier with people you know, but for others who are not as close, it can be awkward.

How has the start been for you?

People often manage their own reaction to your cancer diagnosis with one of two responses:

1  "You are going to do great." "You are so strong." "This is just a bump in the road." "You will look back on this and know that it was only a small blip."

2  "I hope that your treatments go well." "We will hope that God heals you." "I hope you know that many people have overcome this cancer."

Have you every tried inserting "I believe" into your language surrounding your cancer story?

- I believe everything will turn out for me.
- I believe that God loves me and is taking care of me.
- I believe the doctors are doing their very best for me.

Choosing to insert a "believe statement" creates a tone of hope in the midst of your uncertainty. It will be important for you to introduce these strong words of hope into your vocabulary when speaking about your prognosis.

# Discovering New Ideas

*Experience is not what happens to you; it's what you do with what happens to you.*
—ALDOUS HUXLEY

You are likely thinking deeply about the finiteness of life, your family members and even your purpose. In short, you are faced with your mortality.

This is a valley, but you are climbing your way out, day by day.

Already in this unexpected journey you have learned some valuable lessons and gained insights that you did not have prior to your diagnosis.

Today, why not write down some of these nuggets and share them with your family or friends. Don't waste your sorrows. Use them to your advantage.

You can start with, "What I have learned so far in my cancer journey is..." There may be someone who needs to hear the insight that you've gained as a result of this diagnosis.

# Knowing Your Personality Preferences

*Personality is to a man what perfume is to a flower.*
— CHARLES M. SCHWAB

G ive space to those who need to think. Invite those who need to talk with you to do so.

There will likely be people close to you who will take more time to process your diagnosis. They may seem distant or disinterested initially, but in fact, they just need time to come to terms with what is going on. They will come back in due course.

Others will want to talk all the time and openly express their feelings to you. If you are similar to them in your extroversion, you will welcome their openness. If you are more introverted, their expressiveness might be exhausting for you and you'll find yourself craving some space.

Either way, you will need to recognize your personality preferences and understand others who are closest to you.

Most importantly, talk about it and let people know what you need in order to manage your energy. This can be done respectfully, while acknowledging other people's personality preferences.

# Writing Letters

*The way we communicate with others and with ourselves ultimately determines the quality of our lives.*
—TONY ROBBINS

I t's pretty tiring to talk to every single person who is concerned about you.

Once the news gets out about your cancer diagnosis, you will have at least two different types of responses:

1   People who get in touch with you right away and want to know what is going on, and

2   People who are concerned but are afraid to contact you because they don't know what to say.

You will be surprised which of your friends and family fall into those categories.

To save you time and emotional energy, why not write a letter? Yes, perhaps it's a form letter or a group email, but it might be a great way to connect with every member of your extended family or a friend who is at a distance, who needs to hear your news. You will feel better once you communicate with them.

And it will be good for you too — rallying the troops for support and encouragement isn't a bad idea.

# Doing Something for Someone Else

*Never reach out your hand unless you're willing to extend an arm.*

—POPE PAUL VI

There is something empowering about doing something for another person, especially when you are not at your best.

If you are able, choose to do something for someone else today. You might not have the energy or feel your best, but you can build into another person's life in some way.

You can choose a person you know or even a stranger.

If a person has been bringing you meals on your toughest days, perhaps you are at a place in which you are able to reciprocate now. A note of thanks or encouragement from you could really bless someone else.

When you serve and give back, your heart feels glad. It's win-win.

Be creative and do something for someone else today! Your heart will be happy.

# Embracing Humor

*From the stage I've seen people of all ages*
*absolutely roaring at really good toilet humor.*
—ADRIAN EDMONDSON

Regardless of your circumstances, humor needs to find its way into your life. Especially when life throws you a wrench.

During World War II, the German army recognized that the Englishmen's penchant for witty humor was holding the entire British army together in the face of great trauma and they wanted in. Attempts were made to introduce more humor into the German ranks in the hopes that it would fortify the soldiers and make them more resilient.

As the old saying goes: "Laughter is good medicine."

All too often people think that if we are going through a difficult time in our life that we want to keep things somber or serious. While cancer does challenge us to peer into our mortality more intently, it also means that we need more laughter as a counterbalance.

Today why not invite your funniest friend over? Tell him or her you want a good laugh. Choose a movie that makes you guffaw. Read an uproariously funny book. Watch a YouTube video that makes your heart lighter. Watch your favorite stand-up comic either live or on TV.

You can do this by yourself or better yet, do it with your family or friends.

Today is Humor Day…knock knock…

# Talking to God

*The feeling remains that God is on the journey, too.*
—TERESA OF AVILA

Perhaps you've been having some conversations with God already, or maybe not. Most likely you have wondered if there is a God and if this God is near or not. Maybe others have caused you to think about the role of God during this time by their questions.

You may want to seriously consider the place that God has in this cancer journey. Is there something or someone bigger than you? Is this something or someone involved in any way in your cancer journey? It may be time to take a deeper look at the possibility.

Others around you may not be interested in the idea of a being who is both transcendent and personal, but it may be a good step to at least invite the internal conversation to take place and ask the question: "God, are you there?"

# Learning to Create

*Creativity requires the courage to let go of certainties*
— ERICH FROMM

Expressing ourselves in tangible ways can help us to articulate what we are going through on the inside.

Play and creativity will look very different for each one of us depending upon our interests and skills. You may be surprised by your own ability to create something once you start. Or perhaps you are picking up an old hobby that you wished you had had more time for in the past. Now you are in a different place and can make it a priority.

Why not pick up a pen, a paintbrush, a hammer or a guitar and start to create something new today? Share the project with someone else. It always feels good to sit back and enjoy the work of our hands.

# DAY 29:
## Listening to the Music

*Where words fail, music speaks.*
—HANS CHRISTIAN ANDERSEN

For many, music is a powerful medium, a sacred pathway. It does something inside of them that nothing else can do.

Do you have a favorite band or artist whose music connects with you in a way that is especially meaningful?

Today, why not pick your favorite music and play it. It's all at your fingertips online anyway. Listen to it. Engage in the words. Allow the melodies to fill you. Perhaps it's music that reminds you of a certain wonderful time in your life. Or maybe it's time to discover a new artist who seems to come in a back door and express what you are feeling. Regardless, music can help formulate what it is we're feeling.

Why not create a playlist and make music a part of your day if it's not already? When you feel like words cannot express what you are going through, let the gift of music meet something deep inside of you.

And while you're at it—why not sing along at the top of your lungs!

# DAY 30:
## Celebrating Just Because You Should

*Anyone who's just driven 90 yards against huge men trying to kill them has earned the right to do jazz hands.*
— CRAIG FERGUSON

Celebration is the lifeblood of who we are as humans. And celebration is never more needed than when we are going through tough times.

You don't always need a reason to celebrate. Just call this a celebration day and do it up big: cakes, food, balloons, people, family, gifts and decorations. "Just because" goes a long way in making life more fun. Call it a "we-need-to-celebrate-for-no-reason-at-all day" or even give it a specific reason – but make sure you celebrate. There's always a good reason to celebrate if you're grateful for life.

Laugh. Sing. Dance. Eat.

Celebrate!

# About The Author

The author of Finding Anchors, *Taking Notice* and *Looking Ahead*, Rick Bergh was born and raised in Alberta and educated at Augustana University College, University of Alberta, and Saskatoon Lutheran Theological Seminary.

He is a Certified Thanatologist (CT), a designation bestowed by the Association for Death Education and Counseling (ADEC) after rigorous study in the area of death, dying and grief. In addition to his counseling practice, Rick is an author and speaker and has been heard numerous times on national radio.

Rick's various career paths and colorful life experience have given him a unique vantage point in his work as a thanatologist, educator, counselor, speaker and author.

Rick's 30-year vocation as a parish pastor positioned him among people who were continually working out life as a result of normal and unexpected transitions. His practical approach to transition is a result of hundreds of hours spent with individuals who were working through their loss, both personal and family.

His work in the community over the years as a volunteer, sports coach, community counselor, educator and funeral officiant broadens his knowledge and experience as he engaged people in their everyday challenges, listening and learning from their powerful stories.

His career change from pastor to businessman afforded him the opportunity to travel the world, expanding his awareness of cultural differences and universal truths in the area of loss.

Rick has taken his astute people and business skills and applied them to his work with his clientele, providing practical and effective approaches to his transitional loss work.

His personal journey with his first wife, Pam, who was diagnosed with cancer at the age of 42, dying five years later, has shaped his principles and understanding of loss. He and his four children searched for healthy ways to move forward at a key time in their lives.

Connect with Rick on his popular blogging website (www.intentionalgrief.com), where he shares his thoughts, stories and resources of practical approaches to loss. You can also check out his many other resources at www.rickbergh.com.

Rick Bergh and his wife, Erica, live in Cochrane, Alberta, Canada, in the foothills of the Rocky Mountains.

# CONTACT RICK

To get the latest *Finding Anchors* updates and resources, visit: www.rickbergh.com/findinganchors

Rick speaks frequently on the topics found in his insightful and practical book. He can deliver a keynote, half-day, or full-day version of its content, depending upon your needs. Please visit his speaking webpage at:

**www.rickbergh.com/findinganchors/speaking**

## ANCHOR DOWN

Are you interested in bringing Rick's experience and skills right to your home, enabling you and your family to put down some solid anchors as you weather the storms of a cancer diagnosis?

You've read Finding Anchors and you have worked through Cancer Diagnosis: 30 Tips to Help You Land on Your Feet and you would appreciate a little more guidance, face to face.

Rick's Anchor Down Coaching Program gives your family direct contact with the author to help individual family members.

Pick Rick's brain as a counselor and coach. Whether via Skype or on the phone, the time you spend with Rick will be beneficial. For more details, go to

www.rickbergh.com/ findinganchors/anchordown

All of Rick's resources are available at www.beaconmountpublishing.com

BEACON MOUNT
PUBLISHING

### Taking Notice
How a Cancer Journey Can Magnify What's Important in Life

Transformational ideas are always in demand.

In this powerful book, Rick Bergh suggests that the most difficult challenges in your life are often your greatest teachers. We need to lean into them and learn from them.

Apply Rick's 17 "Lean Into Loss Principles" to any life transition and come out the other side with hope and a sense of new direction in your journey.

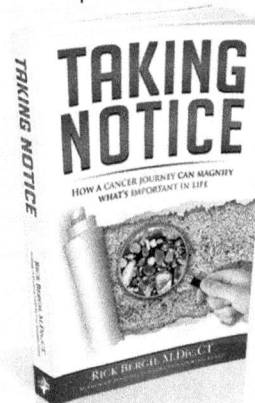

### Looking Ahead
How Your Dying Impacts Those Around You

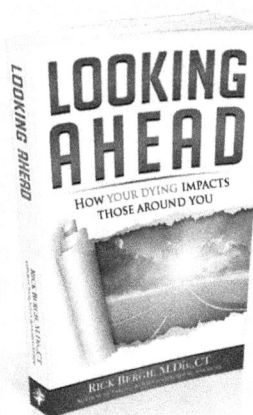

The ripple effect from your dying has a huge impact on those closest to you.

During his wife's final three months on earth, author, Rick Bergh, learned 17 very important lessons. In Looking Ahead he shares a framework for you to consider so that you and your family can make the most of your final days together.

All of Rick's resources are available at
www.beaconmountpublishing.com

Have you read *Finding Anchors: How to Bring Stability to Your Life Following a Cancer Diagnosis*?

Connect with us and tell us your story at
www.rickbergh.com/findinganchors

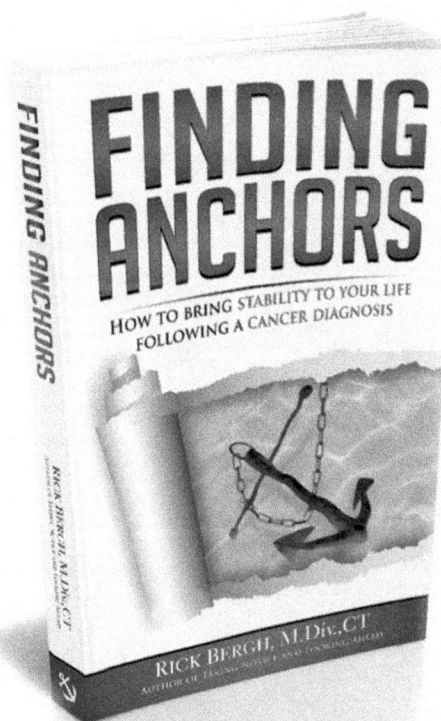

Your free book supplements *Finding Anchors: How to Bring Stability to Your Life Following a Cancer Diagnosis*. You may have already received it as a free gift in digital format by purchasing the *Finding Anchors* book.

It is also available in paperback at
www.beaconmountpublishing.com

# THE FINDING ANCHORS
## DISCUSSION GUIDE SERIES

....reinforce the 17 ANCHORS with one or more from this series of interactive discussion guides.

Whether you are requiring…

- A resource to be used in your home with family
- A guide that will help form a community support group
- An educational tool to help your faith community become equipped
- Material to engage your clients in a counseling setting

…you will find a guide to meet your needs. For more details go to www.rickbergh.com/findinganchors/guides

FAMILY DISCUSSION GUIDE

FAMILY

SUPPORT GROUP

FAITH COMMUNITY

PROFESSIONAL

All of Rick's resources are available at www.beaconmountpublishing.com

Learn more about Rick's transitional loss principles at www.rickbergh.com

BEACON MOUNT